Play the Ball Where the Monkey Leaves it

MINDFULNESS STORIES FOR DAILY LIVING

Francis Valloor

Play the Ball Where the Monkey Leaves it

MINDFULNESS STORIES FOR DAILY LIVING

Francis Valloor

A Division of Maoli Media Private Limited

Play the Ball Where the Monkey Leaves It
Mindfulness Stories For Daily Living

Many of the stories in this book were published earlier in *The Dewdrop in the Ocean*

First Edition: 2017

Published by
ZEN PUBLICATIONS
A Division of Maoli Media Private Limited

60, Juhu Supreme Shopping Centre,
Gulmohar Cross Road No. 9, JVPD Scheme,
Juhu, Mumbai 400 049. India.

Tel: +91 9022208074
eMail: info@zenpublications.com
Website: www.zenpublications.com

Cover:
Detail from the work *'Amazing Grace / Oil on Board'* by Paul McCloskey
Author Photos: El Keegan
Book Design: Red Sky Designs, Mumbai

ISBN 978-93-85902-18-5

Printed by
Repro India Limited

Contents

Foreword

Three years ago when I had a series of eye surgeries, a friend who visited me said, "I suppose we play the ball where the monkey leaves it."

She explained that she had read about a golf course in Calcutta where they were grappling with a serious monkey menace. Try as they might, they could not stop the monkeys from invading the golf course where members played or carrying away the golf balls for their own amusement. Finally the exasperated club owners decided on an addition to the club rules: "We play the ball where the monkey leaves it."

When awareness opens our eyes to see what is there, the gift is the acceptance of how things are. Peace is the outcome of coming to terms with what life brings.

Day-to-day life of chopping wood and carrying water does not stay quite that way but is often punctuated by changes and challenges, toil and turmoil, by surprises and sufferings requiring of us a response that, in fact, shows where we are on the spiritual journey.

When acceptance of reality is our natural way, we have reaped the fruits of awareness. Awareness then turns you into a mystic and you return to daily life.

The stories in this book are based on the themes of daily living. Some of these are from personal experiences but others from the vast wisdom of humanity. You will hear in these stories the echoes of many great sages and mystics from across the world. You may recognise here the wisdom of Ramana Maharshi, Ramesh Balsekar, J Krishnamurti, Anthony de Mello, and many others. The author gratefully acknowledges their contributions to this work which aims to lead to an acceptance of reality in whatever form it comes.

– Francis Valloor
Dublin

Human Nature

Conquest

Someone reported that a new group of mountaineers had conquered Mount Everest.

"How is it that people cannot just climb a mountain?" the sage asked. "Why do they see it as an act of conquest?"

One of the listeners suggested it might not mean anything, just a careless use of words.

"Those words are a statement of human relationship with nature," suggested the sage. "You can conquer a mountain or you can befriend it."

Negativity

A businessman complained he was having problems at work as well as at home. "They say that I'm negative in my attitudes. I've thought about it and there may be some truth in it."

"What are you doing about it?" the sage asked.

"I have tried everything. I have even tried positive thinking, but none of it works!" he exclaimed in frustration, quite unaware of the irony.

Vision

A man who described himself as a failed businessman and parent said he had been unsuccessful in nearly everything he had undertaken. "My life is a struggle," he said, "lurching from one problem to another. I keep dreading when the next problem is going to appear."

"With a belief system like that you can't see your own contribution to the way life has been for you," the sage said. "If you believe life is a struggle, that is what you experience. If you wait for problems you won't be disappointed."

The business man wanted to hear more. The sage continued, "Liken your life to driving a car. Where your eyes go, there the car goes. You don't focus on what the walls or trees on the way that you wish to avoid. Likewise, where your vision takes you, that's where your life goes."

"Surely I can't wish away the failures and problems of the past," the man objected.

"That will be like driving your car with your eyes firmly fixed on the rearview mirror," the sage replied.

Achievement

"In my youth I wanted to become somebody but I never went beyond my clerical post," a grey haired visitor explained. "It took me years to find out who I am and to become somebody."

"Not an easy thing to do," commented the sage. "It is said that Charlie Chaplin won only the third prize in a Charlie Chaplin look-alike competition."

Deals

Seeing a full-page advertisement in a newspaper with a loud banner proclaiming 'FREE!', the sage commented.

"I'm sure there is nothing free there, but people always look for deals that cost nothing."

"What do you mean by that?" asked a friend.

"Expecting peace without inner transformation. Power over people without conflict. Attachment without suffering. Seeing without looking," he replied.

Delusions

The sage would regale his listeners with stories through which he often conveyed difficult concepts. One day he told them of a woman who had walked into a psychologist's office with a German Shepherd on a leash.

"Well?" said the psychologist, "How can I help you?"

"It isn't me, doctor," explained the woman, "It's my husband. He thinks he's a German Shepherd."

The sage then continued, "It's always other people who are deluded and it's their follies that are amusing."

Labels

A middle-aged woman said she and her husband had been married for many years but she would be angry and aggrieved whenever she thought that he didn't respect her belongings or preferences. "He should give me what is mine and I will give him what is his."

"In nature there is no mine and yours," said the sage. "In the mind there is, for it separates, divides and apportions. To tag things as yours and mine is a disease of the human mind."

Assumptions

"Our perceptions are determined by our needs and assumptions," the sage stated.

Someone asked for an example and the sage had one ready.

"An ad in a newspaper read 'What every young woman should know well before marriage. Profusely illustrated. Explicit instructions. Sent in plain wrapper.' Thousands of eager buyers requested the volume. Each one received a very good cook book."

Self-Hate

A man who lived in strict accordance with his religious beliefs was discouraged by what he perceived as his frequent sins and failures. "Everything I do seems to be a mistake. I feel I'm no better than an animal as I've lived a life of sin."

"Self-hatred is a human disease," the sage commented. "Animals don't wallow in self-loathing and self-disgust, do they?"

Perfection

Speaking of the frustrations of human life, the sage once said, "Human beings grieve for the perfect parents they never had. They look for the perfect spouses they will never find."

He went on to tell them about a man who, armed with a shopping list of qualities he desired in his perfect wife, searched high and low for her for many years. He had nearly given up when he finally met the perfect woman who matched every quality in his long list.

"Did he finally marry her?" asked one of the listeners.

"How could he?" replied the sage, "She was in search of the perfect husband."

Humour

In one of his talks to the leaders of a religious organisation, the sage said, "There are some things many religious organisations and despotic rulers have in common. These apply, in fact, to anyone who wields power but lacks a modicum of self-awareness."

"What are they?" asked one of the listeners.

"They crave for more power. They can't take a criticism cheerfully and try to destroy their opponents," he replied. "Above all, they tend to lack a sense of humour."

Parenting

"My little girl is very troublesome," a mother complained. "I'm doing everything to give her a solid upbringing."

"How are you going about it?" the sage asked.

"I get her to go to church in the morning. She gets breakfast only when she comes back. I have her join evening prayers but after 15 minutes, she loses interest and falls asleep. So I sometimes drop a little candle wax on her hands to wake her up. Sometimes I don't talk to her if she disobeys. But mind you, I never beat her."

"And you say it's the little girl who is troublesome!" exclaimed the sage.

Condemnation

A die-hard follower of a religious group that opposed anything worldly, pleasurable and enjoyable was concerned that neither the sage nor others around him shared this attitude.

When the man suggested that they should support his moral crusade, the sage replied, "The proper place to begin is with yourself. You hate what you fear, you preach against what tempts you. You condemn in others what you have difficulty acknowledging in yourself."

"But don't we have a duty to show others the right way?" the man asked.

"You have no duty or obligation to anyone. You have no responsibility for anyone's behaviour or destiny. All you are here to do is to live your own life and realise all that you are," the sage replied as the man looked stunned.

Abandonment

A man described how he had helped many people and he therefore thought he had many good friends. That was until he came up on hard times.

"When I hit a rough patch I was all alone," he recounted sadly.

The sage responded, "When you're alone is indeed the best time to study human nature."

Imagination

An artist was in discussion with the sage about the powers of human imagination.

“Imagination is the glory of humanity,” the artist claimed, “It creates our works of art and heavens in the human mind.”

“Indeed!” the sage agreed and added, “And our hells, too.”

As the artist listened, the sage continued, “Imagination is also what makes you think there is love when there are only strong emotions or you’re having a wonderful time when you’re only spending money.”

Martyr

A woman related that she was going to marry a man who had given up his worldly, wanton and reckless life style after a spiritual conversion. Now he was on a strict spiritual path.

"Marry a saint if you don't mind being unhappy or wish to become a martyr," the sage cautioned. "A sinner recently turned saint can turn into a spiritual terrorist."

Childhood

A man insisted that he would always live by what his parents had taught him and who valued their acceptance more than anything else.

The sage said, "Childhood shoes pinch and misshape your feet. As a child you needed people's acceptance. Now you don't." Then he added, "The trouble with you, my friend, is that you are forgetting that you are no longer that child."

Risks

A middle-aged man said he had inherited the small family business and had kept it on course for 30 years. He admitted that he had not made any profits in all those years.

"I was afraid to take any risks so that I wouldn't end up losing what I had," he said.

"Those who have never hurt their toes may have been immobile," the sage commented. "As in business, so in life; those who do nothing do nothing wrong, but do nothing good either."

Approval

A teacher described how she was overly concerned about other people's approval of her. She worried about the good opinion of other teachers, parents and her students and she would avoid what might upset them.

"That indeed is a handicap that keeps you stuck," acknowledged the sage. "In reality, you don't have to be too concerned about what other people think about you. Most people are, in fact, doing what you're doing. They are thinking about themselves."

Insomnia

A young man spoke about his problem of insomnia caused by persistent thoughts that caused anxiety. He would try to resolve all the issues that caused anxiety so that he could fall asleep peacefully, but hours later he would find himself still awake and frustrated.

"I was taught to examine my thoughts and feelings and go to their roots so that I could be at peace," he said.

"That is like digging to get out of a pit," the sage commented.

Images

The sage once commented that people are quite content with ideas and images and do not necessarily want reality. In fact, images ward off the vision of reality, he said.

As an example he added that one day he said to a woman that her baby was very beautiful. "The mother's reply was," said the sage, 'Oh, that's nothing – you should see his photographs!'"

Revisits

A group of tourists, impressed by the beautiful landscape with a large and serene lake and beautiful wooded hills in the background, set out to take photographs.

"These photos will remind us of our visit here," one of them told the sage, "and we can revisit the place each time we see them."

"If you are fully present and enjoy something once, you will not yearn to go back to it," the sage suggested. "You feel the need to return to experiences you did not complete the first time. Mementos and photographs are only attempts to do that, but they have only partial value."

Relationships

Clinging

A woman spoke about the frustrations in her marriage. "My husband and I have little in common. If we had children we could talk about them. We speak of nothing personal or intimate to each other. In fact, we don't even share our bed any longer."

"What keeps you together then?" the sage asked.

"I guess both of us are scared to face life alone," she said. "Both of us are afraid to be lonely."

The sage said, "Fear is known to hold people together long after love has failed."

Need

A couple said that they loved each other so deeply that they could not bear being separated even for a day.

"What you experience may well be the extent of your loneliness and the strength of your clinging to each other rather than the depth of your love," the sage said.

Purpose

"In my relationship with my husband," said a woman, "I have always tried to put him at the centre. His happiness is my happiness, his joy is my joy. That will bring out the best in him. I think of myself last."

The sage saw it differently. "Let the purpose of your relationships be to bring out the best, the noblest and the most loving in yourself," he said. "So focus on yourself, your goals, your happiness and your joys. That will bring out the best in him, too."

Reflections

A psychotherapist said that the sage's teaching that love begins with oneself was difficult for her to accept. "And when you go on to say that I have to put myself at the centre or love myself first, I find that hard to digest. I may have been trained in the old school that love makes you think of the other first and yourself last."

"Your relationship with yourself is primary and makes all other relationships possible. The first dance, the one that makes every other dance possible, is the one you have with yourself. You can't love another if you don't love yourself," the sage said.

"Relationships are like mirrors. Your love for yourself as well as your self-hate is reflected in your relationships," he continued. "If you love yourself, you love others. If you judge yourself, you judge others."

Avoidance

A man who wished to live like a hermit visited the sage to seek his advice. He wanted to meditate, leaving behind the demands and complications of relationships. "I think relationships only distract me from spiritual pursuits," he said.

"Any realistic spiritual path," said the sage, "has to honour the reality of life and the most basic fact of life is relationships. So, attempting to find freedom by avoiding relationships is like trying to win a game by having only one team."

Completeness

"We are two people but we are half of one another. In our love we complete each other," a newly married man said.

"Nice sentiment, but you can never complete another person or make her happy," the sage said. "If you wish to have a sound relationship, share your completeness with each other, not your need."

Search

"There are too many heartbreaks and too many tears as people search for love and not many find the real thing," the sage said.

"How will they find if they don't search?" a listener asked.

"You find it when you stop seeking because your search takes you away from yourself," the sage replied. "You'll never find in others what you don't see in yourself."

Contribution

A business executive said that he had major difficulties in relationships. "At work I'm disappointed with most people. I rarely see someone who does a good job. At home I'm frustrated because my family does not support me enough."

"It's hard to get people made to your own specifications," the sage said. "The day of freedom is when you begin to see your own role in the difficulties you're facing."

Frustration

A young man was in love with a girl who did not share his amorous sentiments. Marriage was out of the question although he was eager. He had begun to vent his resentment and frustration by badmouthing her to acquaintances and planning revenge. A friend persuaded him to talk to the sage.

"I've never loved anyone like this. I won't let her get away with it," he stated, bristling with anger.

"When love has been frustrated this way, there is a necessary question you have to ask," the sage told him. "If it could turn to hate and revenge, was it love in the first place?"

Teacher

A man complained bitterly about his supervisor, who was ever critical and hard to please and never said a word of appreciation. If it had not been for this one man, it would have been a wonderful place.

"Hail the irker," the sage exclaimed, "for he is your teacher!"

Appreciation

A woman said she was frustrated with the negativity of people she worked with. "Sometimes I look for some support and appreciation from people but it's hard to come by," she sighed.

"What you are not getting from others," suggested the sage, "may well be what you are also keeping back – both, from them as well as yourself."

Educator

A teacher described how he had been in his profession for 15 years. He had developed an innovative method of teaching and was admired for his control of any class. He had a natural gift for discipline and succeeded where many failed.

He wanted to know what the sage thought was the best qualification for a teacher: knowledge of the subject, ability to maintain good discipline, or the ability to achieve good exam results.

"For me," the sage told him, "the most important qualification of an educator ought to be his or her capacity to love, the ability to see the goodness in all children and to bring out the best in them.A good teacher teaches only love, never fear."

Reform

A husband told the sage, "We have everything going for us. I have a good job and we have a decent income. But my wife is always dissatisfied and keeps complaining constantly. If she stopped doing that, I would have some peace."

"Your diagnosis may well be accurate but there is a problem with the prescription. We want other people to change so that our world is a little more comfortable and peaceful," the sage spoke.

"You will find peace only if you come to realise that it is not in your power to change another human being."

Alms

A woman described how she had been involved with a series of men but after a while each would dump her. The more she had needed their love, the quicker they had left her. She was getting older and did not see a way out.

"If you approach people with a begging bowl in hand, you get alms, not love," counselled the sage. "You can't have a strong relationship with someone whose love you need so badly."

Shackles

The highly competent and capable senior manager in a multinational company explained how he valued people's appreciation.

"That helps me do my work well. When my boss is happy with me it makes my day. If he is upset or angry I am down all day. It's the same story at home."

"You have mortgaged your freedom for the appreciation of other people," warned the sage. "You can't live your life based on the reassurance you find in the eyes of another person and still hope to be happy."

Powerlessness

The sage was visited by a woman who worked as a high-powered secretary for a CEO, but was terrified of her boss' angry outbursts when she made even a small mistake. "Every time he is angry, I'm speechless. I'm paralysed. I make even more mistakes than before."

"If you can see that your fear is in your own mind, you'll stop attributing such power to this person," the sage pointed out to her.

"But he is powerful, isn't he?"

"It's you who give him the power to make you cringe," the sage replied. "When you change your thinking you'll see a scared little mouse where you now see a roaring lion."

Strength

A distressed mother complained, "I dedicated my life entirely to my husband and children. I gave up my career so that I could take care of them. I worked hard, did everything for them. I sacrificed my own comfort to make them happy and now they are becoming even more demanding. I don't seem to be doing anything right and when they are unhappy with me, I'm devastated."

"You've been busy pleasing people who refuse to be pleased and they have you in chains," the sage told her. "You wouldn't need to please anyone if you were pleased with yourself."

Memories

Violent, even aggressive in the early years of their marriage, a woman's husband once battered her severely. However, for the last fifteen years, he had been thoughtful and sensitive, with never a harsh word.

"The change in him has been complete," she admitted. "But I still find it hard to leave those painful memories behind."

The sage said, "When you no longer find rewards in remaining a victim, you too will change."

Handicap

A young woman said she was powerless in her family. Her husband and mother-in-law controlled her and she could not advance in her career because of them.

"I'm handicapped by the lack of freedom at home," she said. "If I were free, I could have risen in my professional life. I could have been genuinely happy."

The sage's response was brief: "You yield your power to those you blame."

Self-Sufficiency

A man who had met the sage many times admired his ease with everybody he met. "You have such beautiful relationships with all kinds of people – rich people, powerful people, poor people, humble people, men, women and children. What is the secret of good relationships?"

"Your relationships will be happy and delightful if you don't need anything from the other person," the sage explained.

"That doesn't sound realistic. How can you live like that?" the visitor wondered.

"A lot easier than most people think," the sage replied. "Needing is a mental state. Not needing is freedom that's not of the mind. You're not a hostage to other people's expectations or your own emotional states."

Loneliness

The sage noted that people are so afraid of loneliness that they are willing to give up their freedom for what they hope will bring them some love. So most relationships are only insurance policies against isolation and loneliness.

"Human beings can't live without love, can they?" one of the listeners asked.

"Loneliness isn't cured by love but immersion in life," the sage replied. "When you're busy living life, you're never lonely."

Preparation

A woman told the sage that she had had a series of relationships that had ended in hurt and pain. Some of her partners had been possessive, some uncaring, some harsh. "It is only now I realise that none of that was love."

"Discovering what love is not, is a good introduction to knowing what it is," the sage said.

Givers

"We begin our relationships with great hopes but why do most of them end in failure?" asked a young visitor.

"Most relationships fail because people are convinced that others have something that they need and getting that would make them happy," the sage explained. "That's why givers are few, but takers many; needy enough to take but not full enough to give."

Rules

In a talk on relationships the sage spoke about the madness of society.

"The rules are crazy. If you abide by them, you find assured unhappiness." He named some of the assumptions people carried. "You are nobody until someone loves you. You cannot be happy without some other person's love. If you cry when someone dies, it shows how much you loved the person."

"But what can we do? We have to live in this world," a visitor asked. "My question is, how can we avoid getting hurt and suffering?"

"The world of your relationships is of your own making," replied the sage. "So if you insist on dancing with an elephant in your front garden, you should expect some damages to your lawns and plants."

Aloneness

After her divorce, a woman complained about her loneliness. "Nobody seems to write to me. Nobody invites me for events now. The phone seldom rings and I am stuck at home." She added, "Perhaps you will advise me to go out and make friends with people again."

The sage regarded her kindly and suggested, "Before you do that, I'd advise you to understand and befriend your loneliness. For you'll be lonely as long as you're afraid to be alone."

Knowledge

"I am fair in my judgment of people. I size them up quite quickly based on their behaviours and attitudes," a professor of law said rather proudly. "My love and hate are never irrational but strictly based on my knowledge of people."

"You don't dislike or hate people because you know them," commented the sage, "but because you really don't know them. And once you hate them, you'll never know them. With self-awareness and compassion alone do you understand another; without them you misunderstand."

Volunteer

A business woman in her forties said she had been successful in business but her relationships were marked by unhappiness. "I've had several marriages and partnerships and in all of them I've been unhappy," she said. "I've been let down, abused, betrayed and battered. I'm tired of being a victim time after time." She waited for a few moments and added, "Nobody can say it's my fault."

"You will do well to see your own part in what keeps repeating in your relationships," the sage said. "The first time you may be a victim, thereafter you are a volunteer."

Transformation

A woman who worked in customer service felt resentful and drained out by the demands of co-workers and family members.

"I could appreciate customers and their grievances, but I had difficulty with colleagues and my husband who, too, were pulling out of me all the time as well. When I began to see them also as troubled and vulnerable, I became kind and patient towards them," she said. "The big surprise for me is that now they are easier and kinder towards me."

"You're witnessing how awareness has changed your relationships," the sage remarked. "When the way you see people undergoes transformation, the people you see will experience transformation too."

Dance

A young nurse talked about the difficulties in her relationship with her husband. They were married for nine years and their relationship was being challenged by frequent conflicts.

"We're engaged in this dance and we seem to bring out exactly the same response from each other all these years. The more I give, the less he takes responsibility. The closer I try to get to him, the farther he moves away," she said. "I just don't know what to do any more."

Realising that she was intelligent and insightful, the sage's reply was brief: "Change the dance!"

Honesty

A woman said her husband and she had a troubled relationship. They lived in the same house, had their own lovers, and pursued their separate careers. Lately they no longer fought openly, but a cold war continued interspersed with occasional pleasantries.

"We have decided not to seek a divorce because we thought it would harm our two children," she concluded.

"Your conflict ridden charade is more harmful to your children than divorce," the sage said. "And consider what the legacy you leave your children will be – do you wish them to show hypocrisy or honesty in their own relationships?"

Family

A young couple said their lives were totally centred around their two children. They had decided to suspend their own lives to a large extent until they grew up, they said expecting to be praised for their love and commitment for their children.

"You are ruining your family by centring it on your children. Place your own relationship at the centre and live your own lives and the children join you," the sage said. "Few other things have as much negative impact on children as the unlived lives of the parents."

Suffering

Involvement

The sage was injured in a car crash and had a leg in a cast. One of his visitors asked, "Are you suffering like everyone else or are you somehow spared all that?"

"There is pain but no suffering," the sage replied.

The visitor was intrigued. The sage explained that his body was like anyone else's. When there was an injury, there was bound to be pain, which was a physical phenomenon.

"But then how is there no suffering?" he asked.

"Pain is just pain, but it becomes suffering when the me gets involved in it," the sage elaborated.

Ending

"There is so much pain and suffering in the world," exclaimed one of the sage's visitors. "Is it possible for us to be free from it all?"

"Pain is unavoidable as long as we are alive," the sage answered. "But suffering can be ended and there is only one way to do that – through awareness and understanding."

"Understanding what?" the man asked.

"Understanding how we suffer," was the sage's reply. "That will put an end to suffering."

Relief

"Everywhere people are looking for freedom from their suffering," a visiting psychologist said.

"I don't assume that everyone does," the sage responded. "Most people want some instant relief and consolation, but not freedom. They want to feel good but not necessarily to change."

"But doesn't everyone want to be happy?" the psychologist asked.

"Perhaps everyone does," the sage replied. "However, many people cling to their suffering and don't want to let go of a major source of sympathy. That's the pleasure of their pain."

Spiral

A man had squandered his wealth for several years. He neglected his family, health and well-being. Friends and relatives had tried to help him but he continued on his downward spiral.

“After all our efforts he has not budged one bit and I know he is suffering too,” a close friend acknowledged sadly. “When will he begin to change?”

“Obviously he hasn’t suffered enough,” was the sage’s comment.

Motivation

"Pain is the most dreaded fact of life. It doesn't serve any useful purpose, does it?" a nurse asked.

"Pain is a great motivator for people," the sage responded. "People respond to advice and inspirations with resolutions and promises, but pain they obey."

Happening

The distinction the sage made between pain and suffering was difficult for some people to grasp. He explained that pleasure and pain make up the inevitable duality of life. "But suffering is optional," he added.

They wanted to know more. "Pain is simply a happening," he elaborated. "It's the mind that creates suffering by personalising the pain and by holding on to it."

Flight

A friend asked the sage, "What's the root cause of human suffering?"

"Our reluctance to accept what is," replied the sage.

"And how can we accept what is?"

"By understanding," the sage answered. "For that, you have to face reality and not flee it."

Compassion

A comment that insightful listeners always made about the sage was that he took human suffering seriously and never gave glib solutions to problems.

When asked about the reason for his depth of understanding, he simply replied, "Only sorrow understands sorrow."

Triumph

A university professor was present in the group one day when the discussion turned to suffering. He had suffered much after he had been discredited by accusations of plagiarism. Major financial troubles had added to his problems. In addition, one of his sons had been diagnosed with a severe mental illness.

In the midst of all this he was calm and peaceful and not a word of anger or bitterness would be said against those who had falsely accused him.

"Suffering transforms human beings," commented the sage. "In suffering you see humanity at its best and its worst. Some turn bitter, wallow in self-pity, lose hope and perish. Others surrender and become compassionate even towards the perpetrators."

All were listening intently. After a few moments of silence the sage added, "Ultimately it is not what happens to us, but what happens in us that matters."

Division

The father of a young soldier, a double amputee, was visiting the sage for the third time in one week. "This war has been going on for five years but it came home to me only when my son was injured," the man admitted.

"It's the mind that creates yours and mine, friends and enemies, my country and your country, my suffering and yours. This division is the beginning of war," the sage explained.

The grieving father was listening.

The sage continued, "The belief that our children are more important than the children of other people is the cause of war."

Impersonality

The sage often spoke about the basic impersonality of phenomena because he believed that understanding this would help end our suffering.

"There is nothing personal about the storm that uproots trees or the rain that makes things sprout and grow. An earthquake is impersonal as is the fall of autumn leaves. These are not to please or harm anyone."

"It's certainly hard to say that when it's I who suffer," one of the men said.

"What is not personal is not to be personalised," the sage replied. "It is not my pain or your pain but the pain of the whole world in which we all share."

Moment

"I am overcome by anxiety about my health, financial security, my work and family. I fear that something bad may happen any moment and I am on edge," a businessman said.

"There really is no future. This moment is all there is. And in this moment all is well," the sage said. "Your anxiety cannot coexist with that understanding."

Discovery

A visitor said he had suffered many hardships and difficulties earlier in his life but lately had been spared of similar situations.

"I know those experiences have brought me in touch with truth," he continued. "I keep alive the memory of the pain to help me stay on track."

"The pain may have been necessary for you to discover the truth," the sage observed, "but you don't have to keep living in pain to keep the truth alive."

Problems

A man complained about the troubles and problems in his life.

"Sometimes I wonder if they will ever end. Most of the time they are not big, they are only irritants. Yet I am not at peace. Will I ever be free of them?" he asked.

"Perhaps those irritants will remain," replied the sage. "But while you are waiting, consider this. Oysters use the intruding sand grain irritant to make the precious pearl. What are you doing with yours?"

Attitude

A woman said that her husband was an alcoholic, one of her children was chronically ill and she had major financial problems. Life was difficult and she had been suffering greatly. Her many prayers for freedom from sufferings had not borne fruit.

The sage looked at her with compassion and sat silently with her for a while. Then he suggested gently, "Prayers asking God to change his mind about your life don't bring freedom. Your freedom is in your attitude towards whatever happens in life."

"What's that freedom?" she asked.

"True freedom is in the acceptance of whatever life brings and being at peace whether the situation changes or stays the same."

Duality

The discussion one day was about the pains and problems of life. The sage noted that everything in life is set up as paired opposites - pain and pleasure, masculine and feminine, good health and illness, light and dark, success and failure, and so on.

"Surely life would be so much better if we had only the one side," a visitor said.

"I know which of the two sides you would like to keep," the sage suggested. "However, constant sunshine alone without regular rain ends up creating deserts."

Spirituality

A middle-aged man described how he had been on a spiritual path for many years. He meditated regularly and had had some intense spiritual experiences. Yet when confronted with illness and the death of his wife, he was helpless and depressed.

"I'm questioning the usefulness of my spirituality because I see how unprepared I am to face life," he said.

"You're wise to question. It's in facing suffering that you observe the power of your spirituality," the sage agreed. "The purpose of spirituality is not to help you forget pain but to understand it, so that it, in fact, transforms you."

Emergence

"When can people be said to have handled the pains and hardships of life well?" asked one of the visitors.

"When those experiences have brought out the best in them – inner strength, courage and compassion," answered the sage. "You know the work is done when they are at peace with life and are grateful even for the difficult times."

Outlook

A young man said he was involved in a movement to create a better world. "We hope one day the world will be rid of all pain."

A young woman in the group disagreed that this was unrealistic because pain would always be there with us. "Pain may continue as long as we live, but you can end suffering by changing your attitude to the pain," the sage said. "That's the one freedom that human beings have and that no one can take away."

Flow

"How does a sage deal with pleasure and pain?" one of the visitors asked.

"The sage understands that pleasure and pain are inevitable in the flow of life and never looks for happiness there," the sage replied. "So while other people fight or resist, the sage lets life happen to him whichever way it comes."

Growth

In the small group that visited the sage one day, was a woman who had lost two of her children to leukaemia. She had grieved their loss and her presence radiated peace. She now devoted her time to working with other bereaved parents.

The sage said that pain would come with gifts to those who were prepared to receive them. All experiences could promote our growth but there was nothing as maturing as pain.

"The maturity of suffering is the movement from being an object of attention to becoming the subject of compassion for others who suffer," he added.

Human Spirit

One of the visitors was a human rights activist who had been imprisoned and tortured by the military government of his country. To the amazement of those who listened to him, there was no sign of bitterness or anger in him even towards those who had treated him cruelly. Instead he embodied kindness and compassion.

"Suffering dehumanises some people," the sage commented, "yet in suffering we also witness the triumph of the human spirit which brings out the noblest and the best in human beings," the sage commented.

Then he read out a prayer scribbled on a scrap piece of paper by a concentration camp victim before she was led to her death in the gas chamber:

"Lord, when you enter your glory, do not remember only people of goodwill. Remember also those of ill will. Do not remember their cruelty and their violence. Instead be mindful of the fruits we bore because of what they did to us. Remember the patience of some and the courage of others. Recall the camaraderie, humility, fidelity, and greatness of soul, which they awoke in us. And grant, O Lord, that the fruits we bore may one day be their redemption."

And this time, as on other occasions he read it, the sage was moved to tears.

Identity

A man recounted his difficulties in business and relationships and the many let downs he had suffered lately. "I feel helpless like a cloud that's being tossed about in the wind," he concluded. "I can't see how awareness can help me at all."

"Awareness can indeed help. Stop seeing yourself either as the wind or the cloud," the sage suggested. "Instead see yourself as the sky."

Understanding

After describing to the sage the difficulties, hardships and sufferings of his life – much of it because of his enemies – the CEO of an organisation concluded, "I wouldn't have understood the problems and struggles of other people were it not for what I have gone through in my own life."

"This is a precious lesson in compassion," the sage observed. "If we could, in fact, hear the life stories of people, including those of our enemies, we would see that there is enough sorrow and suffering to disarm all our hostility."

Roles

A woman who worked for the poor and oppressed sections of society told the sage that because of the stances she had taken, she was herself a victim of abuse and injustice. She recounted some of her horrible experiences while the sage listened silently.

"I've often felt abandoned even by God and wondered where God was when I was treated so badly," she said. The sage was reluctant to speak. Since the woman insisted on hearing his view on such suffering, he found an answer for her.

"Life is a cosmic game in which Consciousness or God works through some people as perpetrators and through others as victims. It's the one reality and we're all merely playing our respective roles."

A little later, he added, "That's why those who see this can appreciate the words of the Hindu scripture: Thou art the speaker and Thou art the listener. Thou art the doer and Thou art the experiencer."

Helping

Compulsion

Wherever she went, a social worker would be looking out for people to help. “I don’t spare any effort to help. That’s what gives some meaning to my life,” she explained.

“Helping without discernment isn’t beneficial to others and you’ll end up frustrated,” the sage warned.

“How do I know when to help and when to hold back?” the woman asked.

“Before you help anyone, always ask this question: ‘Whose need am I meeting – theirs or mine?’”

Self-Help

The sage was known to be compassionate to people who suffered.

At the same time he refused to help those who would not do their part to resolve their problems. He would be direct and unsparing in his responses to them.

"Sometimes compassion comes in the form of a kick in the rear," is how he would explain his approach.

Giving

Parents from working class backgrounds wanted the best for their children. They worked hard, deprived themselves of many comforts and saved money so that the children would not experience the same hardships and deprivations as they had. They gave the children whatever they demanded and allowed them to do whatever they wanted.

The children grew up without any sense of responsibility and their demands kept escalating.

"We did everything for them and gave them all they asked for," complained the parents when they visited the sage. "We don't know why they have turned out this way."

The sage told them, "What the children needed was love, but you gave them things. When they needed limits, you gave them license."

Sacrifice

A religious woman who worked tirelessly for the poor and sick people in her town said that her love for God was the motivation for all her service to them.

"For my love of God I'm prepared to sacrifice everything, my comforts and even happiness. My motto is give, give until it hurts," she said.

"My suggestion is, don't give if it hurts. For love does not demand sacrifices for they would breed resentment towards the poor and God and make you unhappy," the sage said. "Love brings joy and pleasure in all its giving. Perhaps you have heard that God loves a cheerful giver."

Pedestal

A monk lived an austere life. His motivation was to set a good example for others. People revered him as a holy man.

One day when some of his visitors were praising such saintly behaviour, the sage disagreed with them.

"Giving a good example to other people," warned the sage, "is a game of one-upmanship as you set yourself above them. It's also a double-edged sword because if you seek people's veneration, you must be prepared to be despised too. "Besides you can't live on a pedestal and still hope to be alive."

Charity

A wealthy man who had helped many people in need was perplexed by the ingratitude of the beneficiaries. “After all I’ve done, I’m afraid my help has created distance in many relationships. In fact, I’ve lost some good friends.”

“Charity is a risky business because it can dehumanise by depriving the poor and the needy of their dignity,” the sage replied.

“How then am I to help anyone?” the man asked.

“Help from the fullness of your heart rather than the abundance of your wealth,” the sage suggested. “For it is your love alone that will make it easy for people to forgive you for the good you are doing for them.”

Resentment

A doctor spent long hours offering free medical aid in the city slums. For many years he had spent all his waking hours tending to the poor and needy patients without charge.

He added that he felt unable to say no to any request for help because that would make him feel guilty. Now he was burnt out and resentful that the people he had helped were hardly grateful and he felt used.

"If your giving is motivated by needs or compulsions and avoidance of guilt feelings, you will resent the help you give," the sage commented. "And today's helper becomes tomorrow's victim."

Addiction

A school teacher explained that she was addicted to pleasing people. "I have made a career out of pleasing others. I do it with my husband and children. I do it with the principal and kids in my school. Everywhere I go I do too much, give up my own comfort and time to make other people happy and when someone is disappointed, I am devastated."

"Relationships based on the need to please are never happy. They turn you into a victim," the sage remarked. "But seeing that you are a slave is the beginning of your freedom."

Independence

A mother explained that she loved her only son so much that she would help him in every way. She would accompany him to school and help him with his homework, especially maths problems.

"In order to mature, children need to experience difficulties at first hand. Indiscriminate helping will only stunt your son's growth," the sage told her. "Never do for anyone what they can do for themselves."

Guilt

A businessman said he led groups of people abroad to help people living in dire poverty. After his return, he found it increasingly difficult to enjoy even the basic comforts he and his family were accustomed to. When he went out to have dinners with business partners and friends, he would feel guilty. "Here we are enjoying all these luxuries when so many people are hungry and sick. I can't enjoy these things any longer," he told the sage.

"When guilt deprives you of enjoyment, you neither serve the poor nor yourself," the sage replied. "Right actions are never motivated by guilt but the realisation that the poor and you are one, they are not separate from you."

Healing

A counsellor who listened to the sage on a number of occasions said he used to place himself a notch or two above the people he helped. "I have until recently seen myself as a helper and healer but I realise now, as I listen to people and their problems, that they and I are quite alike. I am no better than them," he said.

"When you realise that the people who come to you are telling you your own story, you know then that your own healing is happening," the sage commented.

Consequences

A father was talking about his son who often got into discipline problems at school. However, he would use his influence to bail the son out of trouble.

"I love my son too much to see him punished at school," he clarified.

"That approach will only ruin your son's life," the sage warned him. "If you really loved him, you wouldn't rescue him from the consequences of his behaviour."

Pleasing

A computer engineer said that even after a full day's work he was always on call because his friends would ask for help and he could not say no to them.

"I end up feeling fed up with myself for saying yes to all callers," he complained. "They do not seem to realise I am tired and I am angry with them for using me."

"Most people look out for their own needs. It is no use expecting them to understand," the sage advised. "As long as you can't say an honest no to your friends, you'll resent helping them. They won't respect you and your relationships will be ruined by the very help you give."

Debts

At election time, a politician who visited the sage declared that he was committed to helping and serving the poor. In fact, he had helped a large number of people in his area and now hoped with their help to come to power.

"If the poor are your stepping stones to success, you're only using them," the sage remarked.

The politician was horrified because he had not seen it that way. Besides, he had valued his relationships with those he cared for. So he asked the sage to explain it further.

"Power makes relationships unequal and unstable even if it's the power to help someone," the sage clarified. "If others owe you a debt for something you've done for them, it harms your relationship with them."

Responsibility

In discussion with a group of voluntary workers in a disadvantaged area, the sage cautioned, "Take care how you help those in need. Much of the help people receive keeps them stuck in the victim mode."

"How can we help differently?" one of the volunteers asked.

"You help them most by putting them in touch with their own responsibility," the sage replied.

Challenge

A woman who had been divorced for seven years spoke about her marriage that had lasted ten years and the abuse and violence she had suffered during that time. She would tell her tale of tears to anyone who cared to listen.

"You can stay stuck as a victim and reap the fruits of your past pain in the sympathy of other people," the sage told her. "But people who offer you sympathy and support now are not necessarily your friends; they may be keeping you stuck in your victim role."

"Who are my friends then?" she asked.

"Your friends are those who challenge you to change the story line from now on, to take charge and move on with your life," the sage continued.

Cost

A young wife explained that she had turned down opportunities for higher education to put her husband through medical school.

"I love him so much that I am prepared to give up my own career," she declared proudly.

"Listen deeply to yourself before you help even someone close to you at a cost to yourself," the sage warned. "Otherwise you risk becoming resentful and jeopardising your relationship."

Discernment

People knew the sage as unsparing in his efforts to help those in need. Yet he would insist that helping others has to be done with considerable wisdom and discernment. When asked about wise helping, his message was clear:

Help only those who, in fact, need your help.
Help only those who are willing to help themselves.
Help only those you are happy to help.
Help with the awareness of the impact of your help.
Help in ways that set people free, not bind them in any way.
Help others in ways that allow them to enrich you also.

Intrusion

A psychotherapist told the sage that she cared deeply for the people who came to her but she was unable to help them. Some became dependent and others moved away.

"When you attempt to help without respecting the inwardness of people, they will not trust you," he said. "It is a vital lesson to learn how not to intrude, how not to control and how not to guide another through your own insights."

Authority

Subservience

"Human beings do not grow up and come into their own as long as they are subservient to authorities," stated the sage.

"Without authority there will be chaos," a visitor objected. "Surely we have to heed traffic cops and civil authorities," a listener argued.

"Of course, we need external authority for a harmonious civic system," the sage agreed. "But as long as you are a slave to the internalised authority of others, your growth is stunted. You remain a child."

Forgetfulness

"It's a rare human being who stands tall and walks free and is not led by other people," mused the sage.

"Is it our fault or that of the people in authority over us that we remain followers?" asked one of his listeners.

"It's nobody's fault. It's your forgetfulness," the sage replied. "You follow others only because you forget that you have, in fact, grown up."

Conformity

A visiting social scientist commented on the persistence of harmful beliefs and people's loyalty to authoritarian systems.

"What surprises me is how even intelligent people become uncritical conformists," he continued. "And how even people who faithfully practise their religion can be made to commit the most horrendous crimes against other people."

"No surprise there," the sage commented. "If people can be indoctrinated to believe in the nonsensical, they can surely be brainwashed to commit brutalities."

Obedience

A man who had spent several years as a monk said those years in the monastery had made him obedient. "Whatever else my shortcomings, I learnt to obey others, even those who were below me. In that was my freedom."

"Obedience is a part of the human condition," the sage remarked. "The slave obeys other people but the free man obeys himself."

Realism

A man said he was fortunate that on a recent trip abroad he had found a perfect and fully liberated spiritual teacher who was free from human failings and shortcomings.

"What good will that do for you, my friend?" the sage asked. "Perhaps you believe liberation is freedom from mistakes."

"I was disillusioned by teachers who fell short in their own lives," the man persisted.

"They may indeed fail and fall," the sage continued. "Your own freedom comes when you can see them also as human beings who err, and not keep them on pedestals."

Maturity

"What is the biggest challenge in human life?" asked a young visitor.

"Leaving home," replied the sage.

"What is the biggest challenge in the spiritual life?" an older questioner wanted to know.

"Leaving home," was the unexpected answer.

Discipleship

The sage would often refer to the spiritual genius of the Buddha who rejected inner authority, traditions, scriptures, priesthood and rituals. "In fact, you can't even have a Buddha to follow, for the moment you rely on anything outside of you, you have created an authority to live your life for you."

"Isn't it a bit too much for us to hope to become a sage like you?" asked a visitor.

"A sage doesn't come from another world," he replied. "A sage is someone who has become a light unto himself."

Experience

One of the seekers asked the sage. "What makes a sage free when the rest of us are stuck with all sorts of authority ruling over us and we are afraid to break free?"

"When your freedom comes from your own experience, you follow no one," answered the sage. "And you no longer need to refer to tradition or quote the scriptures."

"When does that happen?" he queried further.

"When your eyes open," replied the sage.

Opportunities

The leader of a spiritual centre said he had large numbers of people attending his programmes. "Most people look for clarity and that is what I offer through structure and what is expected of them.

"More people want to hear you rather than listen to themselves, more interested in being told what to do instead of being led by their own inner light," the sage commented. "Be the leader of a place that offers opportunities and not obligations for people."

Questioning

"What is a wise response to authority?" a seeker asked the sage.

"Questioning," the sage responded at once. "Question even your own experiences," he added. "Seek to be clear sighted in your ecstasies, alert in your darkness, and discerning towards every call to your loyalty."

Learning

Some of the disciples would faithfully write down everything the sage spoke.

One day he told them, "These words are useless without the space between them. If you understand that, my dears, you won't bother to take down everything I say."

Integrity

The sage once told a group of visitors how some years earlier he had faced a major financial crisis and had to live very frugally. He had continued to speak up against unjust authority and some unwise government policies of the day. An acquaintance of his who thrived on his political contacts had a helpful suggestion.

“Learn to be a little subservient to the local leader and you won’t have to live so frugally,” he suggested.

“Learn to live frugally,” the sage countered, “and you won’t have to be subservient to the leader.”

Justification

"Is there any sure way of discerning when authority is unhealthy or harmful?" asked a listener.

"When authority claims divine sanction, you can be sure it is insecure and fear based," replied the sage. "And when it sees itself as being beyond questioning."

Direction

A man said he had looked to religion to provide answers to life's vexing problems. After many years of faithful practice and listening to sermons and discourses, he felt let down.

"All my life I have trusted my religious teachers but they have failed me. For the first time in my life, I feel lost and without direction," he said.

In reply, the sage showed him a newspaper cartoon, which showed a little child stumbling over some stones on the road. With a look of hurt surprise on his face, he asked his mother, "Mummy, why don't you look where I'm going?"

Safety

A religious leader visited the sage to seek his advice. Their discussion turned to religious authority.

"In an insecure world we need someone to tell us what is safe to believe and practise. Otherwise there will be utter chaos. People will pick and choose what they believe and practise and end up with a cafeteria religion," the leader proposed.

"It depends on how you see your role," the sage responded. "You have to make up your mind if you want to be the curator of a museum or cultivator of a garden. In the latter, it may look like chaos from the outside because you don't have complete control over anything that grows."

Inside-Out

The sage's insistence that the primary place of working for freedom from authority was within oneself was a dampener for some. It was so much easier to work on someone other than oneself.

"If you don't start with yourself, you'll only convert your inner conflicts into external battles," the sage made clear. "Surely fighting oppressive powers has borne fruit in history," one of his listeners argued.

"History holds the starkest lesson you will learn about this process," the sage replied. "Unless you start with yourself, you only replace one system or authority with another, often more oppressive and tyrannical than the first."

Rebellion

A visitor had lived all his life as a rebel and now in his middle years he was still revered by many young people as an icon and inspiration for his untiring fight against authority.

He had hoped to find support for his views from the sage but the sage disappointed his expectations, "There is no freedom in defiance and rebellion. You have only frozen in battle mode."

"Surely there is freedom in this. I'm not controlled by others," insisted the man.

"You're never free from what you fight against," the sage said. "In fact, you remain trapped in your relationship with them even though it's adversarial."

Dependence

The sage was at pains to explain to some of his listeners that questioning authority in one's life was not a personalised battle against people in power. It was discovering one's own inner authority.

"Where do we begin?" asked a visitor.

"Look at your need to belong," replied the sage, "your need to depend, your craving for approval, your shame when you don't measure up, your guilt when you fail and your fear of being alone."

Security

"How does authority survive in spite of all the revolts and rebellions against it?" a visitor asked.

"As long as human beings look for security and reassurance, they will create and obey rules, traditions and scriptures," the sage replied.

"Is there any hope for change?" the visitor followed up his question.

"Not as long as human beings are fearful and prefer the security of childhood to growing up to be adults," the sage said.

Control

Weapon

When the sage spoke one day on control as a tool that many leaders used, a religious leader admitted that he had seen it as his only way to run his organisation.

"For me it was not a tool but a weapon: not a preferred one, but the only one. Now I see that it has only bred chaos and resentment, and people haven't learnt to take responsibility."

"Seeing the harmful effects of control is itself liberating. What you control ends up controlling you," the sage said. "It is important to learn the art of teaching without dictating, leading without coercing, and helping without disempowering."

Observation

"How does one bring awareness into organisations?" a business consultant asked the sage.

"By observing what is going on."

"Don't we do that all the time?"

"Most of us view situations through the prism of prejudices, opinions and theories. Seeing directly what is going on gives us direct answers that are obviously simple and surprisingly overlooked."

Reputation

A film star who visited the sage said he had worked hard and built up a reputation which he now had to protect. "I have a firm that is paid big bucks to protect my reputation. I must say my freedom and simplicity of life have been lost."

"A life based on the approval and disapproval of people is full of anxiety," the sage said. "Your need to protect your reputation becomes your loss of freedom. Go beyond good name and bad name and your freedom of action and thought are not impaired."

Legacy

A man in his thirties said throughout his childhood and teenage years his fights with his angry and authoritarian father had made life miserable for him.

"Deal with your father wound," the sage suggested. "Otherwise your conflict with your father will taint your other relationships too."

The man smiled in recognition because he was having difficulties with his boss and anyone else in power. Yet he protested, "My father has changed a great deal since my childhood. He is a very kind and loving towards his grandchildren."

"The father at home may have changed," the sage replied, "but not the one in your head. He is the one who controls you."

Education

A high school teacher said that with each passing year he found the students increasingly difficult to manage. "I came into education with all my ideals of love and teaching but the students are so inured to discipline and control," he said.

"If discipline and control are your means to educate children, you will make no headway in your work," the sage said. "You can't be present to what you seek to control, you can't love what you try to subdue."

Reversal

A politician holding high office remarked condescendingly, "I see that most people are like sheep. For all their protests, the moment there is a show of strength, they fall in line."

"You're mistaken, my friend," the sage corrected the politician. "Study history or simply open your eyes and see. The gentle prevail over the powerful, spirit subdues force, and shows of power are only the masks of insecurity."

Power

The group that gathered one morning talked about the harmful effects of control in people's lives. A senior journalist said that power and aggression were the obvious ways people have controlled other people. "That applies to a whole range of people from mothers-in-law to dictators," he added.

"Those are certainly the obvious ways. But there are subtler and stronger ways of control," the sage noted. "People control quite effectively through helplessness, illness, guilt, niceness and sweetness, too."

Appearances

The president of a business organisation doubted if he had made the right decision in the appointment of a new CEO. He had been billed to be eminently suitable for the job but was gentle and quiet. "For a turbulent time such as this, perhaps we needed an aggressive go-getter," he wondered aloud.

The sage who knew the CEO spoke: "Appearances are famously deceptive. Gentleness is more effective against resistance than aggressiveness. Control and coercion may achieve short term goals but at the cost of harmony and peace."

Aggression

A businessman said he had been for years branded as aggressive go-getter who became successful but at the cost of peace of mind, health and relationships. "I have acquired what money and drive can acquire but I am an unhappy, restless human being and I'm never at peace," he said.

"If peace is what you want, prefer then a quiet, gentle and mindful life," the sage suggested. "The aggressive way ends in discord, disturbance and distraction but the gentle way leads to peace and harmony with others. Then you will find within you the calmness you seek."

Mastery

The head of a business organisation expressed his frustration that in spite of his relentless efforts and the control of his forceful personality, not a whole lot of his goals were being accomplished.

"At this stage I feel like I'm on a treadmill, I'm not getting anywhere but I can't stop it either. How does a sage accomplish so much yet appearing to do so little? Is self-control the secret of success?"

"The sage doesn't control himself, nor is he out of control," replied the sage. "Mastery is self-expression, so his authority comes from who he is, not from his control over people and situations. He knows less is more and a great deal comes out of very little."

Tragedy

A widow described her life as a tragedy, totally controlled by her husband. First it was through aggressive behaviours. Later it was through sweetness and helpfulness. Finally it was through his prolonged illness.

"I'm filled with anger towards him for what he did to me," she said. "But now that he is no more, I'm free."

"Even a dead husband controls you," said the sage, "until you're free from your anger."

Trust

A businessman told the sage that he ran a tight ship and kept a close tab on his employees; he also made it clear that he paid them well.

"I'm not sure of the reasons, but I don't think even after all these years I've gained their loyalty and trust. Until now I was convinced it was their ingratitude, but there may be something that I don't see," he wondered.

"Controlling and managing people cause resistance and distance," the sage explained. "If you understand deeply, you will soon realise that your trust engenders their trust, that loyalty begets loyalty."

Success

"How can I be a successful in my new role?" a young CEO asked.

"By being fully present."

"Does that mean I have to be everywhere and micromanage?"

"That would be impossible and inadvisable," the sage responded. "Being present is first of all being with yourself. Then you'll see clearly, understand deeply and act courageously."

Paradox

The newly appointed principal of an old and prestigious college told the sage that he was struggling in his new role as he felt he had to show quick results. He realised that in his efforts to prove himself he was pushing and controlling his subordinates.

"Let me sum up the paradox of leadership for you," the sage responded. "Desperate need to succeed leads to sure failure. Trying to control creates chaos. Wanting to be strong weakens you."

Inversion

The sage was approached with an invitation by leaders of a major organisation to speak to them about change through awareness. "We have set some specific goals for ourselves and we need your help to accomplish them."

The sage proposed two considerations before accepting their invitation. "Firstly, the change that comes about because of my work may not be along the lines you expect but may be just what is necessary."

"All right, what is the second?"

"Awareness demands that all changes have to begin with you."

He was not contacted again.

Repression

A deeply religious man said he had managed to stay on the religious path by keeping himself "on the straight and narrow." That, he believed, was the only way he could be an agent of change and freedom in the world.

"People use control to bring about change and to prevent change but neither of these works," the sage said. "You are not free because what you control controls you. And people who are controlled are not necessarily fit for freedom but for repression or rebellion."

Self-Awareness

At a conference on leadership, a participant suggested that intelligence and confidence were the most important qualities of leaders.

The sage agreed that they were certainly important but any authority that leaders exercised would have to be rooted in their relationship with themselves.

"To lead oneself is always more difficult than leading others," he observed.

Asked to elaborate, he continued, "Knowing other people requires intelligence, knowing yourself takes wisdom. Leading others calls for authority, leading yourself requires clarity and self-awareness."

Fear

The owner of a successful technology firm attributed his success to the tight control he had over every process and person on campus where “not a molecule was allowed to move without permission.” Of late, some chinks had developed in the system of control leading him to question his approach. He wondered what would make him resort to such control.

“Fear,” said the sage. “Fearful people control, they do evoke fear in others. But if you’re fearless and free, you’re confident and you create an entirely different atmosphere.

“You set people free and bring out the best in them. You don’t stifle initiatives. You respond to situations instead of reacting to your fears. So you set yourself free, too.”

Price

A scholarly monk said after years of living a celibate, austere and restricted life, he felt let down that the promised happiness and spiritual joy had never arrived. "To be honest, life has been tense and full of conflicts and I see no end to it."

"Control is the default mode for dealing with what is threatening," the sage said. "So you have to control your body, emotions, sexuality, thoughts, imagination."

"But we have done this for so many centuries," the monk said.

"And you still haven't learned the lessons," the sage was quite direct. "Anyone who has used control as a way to holiness or happiness and to deal with the challenges they face will know how futile it is as a strategy. And where it seems to work, you pay a heavy price."

Non-Doing

A business leader spoke about the unprecedented upheaval in his organisation. He had tried to analyse the situation and apply the remedies suggested by experts, but they had not worked.

"Your stillness is the surest solution for your organisation's turmoil. So use your awareness as the most basic and reliable tool for your work," the sage responded.

"Perhaps I have to begin meditating," the businessman joked.

"Only choose one that involves seeing what is happening," the sage added. "You'll thus master the art of understanding deeply without analysing endlessly, and achieving much without doing a lot."

Acceptance

Demands

A high school teacher was quite intense in his speech and attitude. After listening to the sage for a while he realised, "I want peace more than anything else, but I see how disturbed I am in life. It's as if wherever I turn something upsets me: I turn on the TV or read the papers, I'm upset. I talk to people, I get annoyed. I go to work and there is no peace."

"The primary reason for your disturbance and disquiet is your demand that reality be different from the way it is," explained the sage. "The moment you accept the way things are, you're at peace."

Attitude

A kind-hearted politician spoke about the recent political reverses and financial losses he had experienced. He was dejected and hopeless as he spoke to the sage. "All my efforts have been thwarted so far," he said. "Is it worth struggling anymore?"

"You have to do everything you're able to do, knowing that your efforts may succeed or fail," said the sage. "Then your struggle can end quickly and your work continue without struggle."

None the wiser for the response he got, the politician asked, "How will that happen?"

"Your freedom is in your attitude," said the sage, "so that you're at peace regardless of the outcome."

Rules

"You say that awareness means acceptance. How does that happen? Are there some rules or guidelines to get there?" a young legal professional asked.

"The first big rule of awareness is to accept what life brings," the sage replied. "The second is to challenge what comes. The third is the most difficult, how to distinguish between the first two."

Success

An author whose book was rejected over 60 times said, "I've heard many famous authors have had such experiences, but to be honest I find that difficult to live with. At this stage I wish I had some success."

"For some people success is finding recognition , for some it is avoiding being discovered," was the sage's cryptic comment.

Resignation

A woman who had multiple sclerosis was distraught as she spoke about her deteriorating condition and the radical change in her health and lifestyle. "I can't accept this because if I stop fighting it and giving in, the disease wins and I lose."

"Acceptance is not welcoming the disease and resignation is not the way forward either," the sage said.

"But what is the difference? I don't see any," she said.

"Acceptance is surrender to life not to the disease, resignation is giving up. Acceptance is inner strength, resignation is powerlessness," the sage replied. "In resignation you try to change the circumstances and fail, but in acceptance you work on your attitude and succeed."

Resistance

A religious man said he had struggled with sexual feelings for many years and though he had resisted those temptations, he had found it too stressful a way to live. He wondered if he would ever find freedom from this.

"Denial of life and its impulses is never the way to joy and peace," the sage said. "Indulgence is not the alternative. But find a way to accept all of who you are. Work with life, not against it. Work with reality, not in opposition to it. In that, you will find a peace that is not easily assailed."

Pressure

A woman said she was thoroughly frustrated in her relationship with her husband who was unpredictable, inconsiderate and hot-tempered. "To be fair he is quite loving and helpful most of the time," she added. "But the contrast is very difficult and I'd like to see him change."

The sage replied, "Beginning with a demand that he changes is rejection and criticism and he reacts to it. Begin with an acceptance of him and the outcome is likely to be different."

"Does that mean I have to agree with his ways?"

"Acceptance is not agreeing with him or condoning his behaviours but the first step to change what you have to deal with," the sage said. "So begin without judgments, giving up your demand for him to be different from the way he is. Be willing to let him be which removes the pressure on him to change. That offers him a better chance to change.

Acceptance

Everyone who met the sage, sensed the unmistakable peace that he radiated. He maintained his equanimity even in periods of upheavals in his country or when he faced stiff opposition for the stances he took.

"How do you remain peaceful even when everything around you is spinning?" someone once asked him.

The sage replied, "I realise that everything is just as it is meant to be. Nothing happens out of turn, everything in its own time, and nothing is out of place," the sage replied. "So there is complete acceptance of whatever life brings. There is no fight against reality, no fear and no regrets."

Options

A middle-aged nurse said that she found working conditions difficult with long hours, gossipy co-workers and demanding superiors. "To make matters worse the pay scale has been cut and it's difficult to make ends meet," she said.

"Things are exactly the way they are if you like them. Things are the way they are even if you don't like them," the sage said. "When the options are so narrowed you might as well make peace with reality and find some peace."

Assent

A lawyer turned businessman who faced many reverses and setbacks said he had become so used to things going wrong that he hardly expected success, peace and happiness in life. "I know I am pessimistic," he said. "Sometimes I ask 'what next?', fearing that more trouble is on its way and I'm going to be stuck this way for the rest of my life."

"Life does not ask for your consent or concurrence in what happens but it cannot make you happy or unhappy against your own assent," the sage suggested. "For that, begin by accepting what is, and you will find peace."

Feedback

A bank executive said that colleagues at work had given him some feedback that he was dictatorial, insensitive and unapproachable. He found this hard to accept.

"You have much to gain by befriending the truth however harsh it may be," the sage said. "Accept what seems unacceptable, turn the harsh truth into an ally and teacher, then you learn and your life changes."

Steps

"We've been married 21 years and I have struggled with my husband's harshness, aggressive ways, insensitivity and miserliness," a middle aged woman said. "I have cajoled, pleaded, threatened and even got him to go for psychotherapy but he hasn't changed one bit. I just can't take it any longer."

"When you set out to change him, it is helpful to see your judgement and rejection which is met with conflict and resistance. If acceptance is the first step, other steps will follow from it," the sage suggested.

Violence

"The founder of our religious group taught us that a resolute fight against our own inclinations, never slackening in our efforts, and never tolerating our own weaknesses are the ways to spiritual growth. I had to work hard at this but I feel I am now the master of my own life," a religious man said.

"That's a sad and uncertain way to live because if you gain a victory through violence, you have to be always on guard and always in battle mode. If the enemy is yourself, fighting and resistance are stupid," the sage replied. "The greatest spiritual accomplishment is the acceptance of all things as they are. Peace of mind is the condition that follows."

Serenity

A visitor asked the sage how he managed to remain peaceful and serene even under adverse circumstances.

The sage replied, "Life is lived with the total acceptance that everything is just as it is meant to be. So there is no regret, fear or anxiety."

As the questioner tried to understand this simple response, the sage added, "There is great freedom in the absence of any judgment of self or other people because of the understanding that nobody does anything. Everything happens on its own."

Hope

"The difficulties of my life have been too many to mention. I have suffered much but after listening to a famous preacher, I have found hope as my source of strength. But I must admit that I am not really at peace."

"The trouble with hope is that it is about the future and, therefore, it is illusory. Acceptance is present, so it is real and you experience it in the present," said the sage to the surprised man. "So give up hope and come to acceptance."

Freedom

Attractions

A young seeker had lived an ascetic life. Believing that alcohol was dangerous to his spiritual pursuits, he was happy to be free from that obstacle.

Yet seeing some of his friends enjoy a drink or two, he was curious. Caught between the two pulls he sought the sage's advice.

"If you can enjoy something without guilt," advised the sage, "and abstain without compulsion, then you're free."

Oppression

A middle-aged monk explained that early in life he had given up sex and the possibility of a family in order to take up a life of prayer and meditation. However, life was a torture sometimes, as sexual desires and images often assailed him.

The sage asked, "Why then did you take up such a way of life?"

"I believed that this was the best way to find God and serve him," the monk replied.

"You never find freedom and happiness when denying your deepest impulses," warned the sage. "And it's a strange God who is served by the denial of something that is basic, natural and life-giving."

Readiness

A young man was distressed about his relationship with a woman. "I love her with all my heart and I can't imagine life without her," he claimed. "But she doesn't seem to care about me."

"You'll have better results if you leave her free to care about you," advised the sage.

"But then I may not get her affection at all," he replied.

"Love is a flower that blooms only in freedom," explained the sage. "You're ready for it only when you're free from the need for someone's love."

Renunciation

A wealthy man said that in his youth he had resolved that at the age of fifty he would free himself from the world by renouncing everything and devoting his life entirely to God and in three months he would turn fifty.

"Renunciation is a dicey deal," warned the sage. "Instead of setting you free, it binds you to what you give up. You miss what you renounce and think about it all the more."

"Does that mean I should live a life of pleasure and indulgence?"

"Live naturally," the sage answered, "That's freedom. Let what you don't need drop off spontaneously but don't give up anything wilfully, not even for God's sake."

Extremes

Some were intrigued by the sage's life and teaching. On the surface there was nothing that appeared extraordinary about him. He did not fit into any mould. He did not recommend austerities and long hours of meditation. He did not teach the denial of pleasures or the embrace of penances. "Freedom is not found in extremes," he would say.

"But isn't it the mark of spiritual strength to give up something like alcohol or sex completely?" a visitor asked.

"It's far easier to give up something completely than to find a wise and comfortable relationship with it," acknowledged the sage.

Patterns

A celebrity who visited the sage said his first marriage had ended after an acrimonious legal battle. Now he and his second wife were parting ways after four years of endless discord and arguments.

"I know I'm a free man and I can change my relationship story. I'll be marrying a good-natured woman I have come to love," he said. "It's going to be different this time. We'll have a happy life together."

"To make that possible, you have to look at what keeps repeating in your relationships," the sage advised. "When you bring awareness into your life that shows you the extent of your slavery to those patterns, you've taken the first step towards your freedom."

Trauma

A forty-year-old woman talked to the sage about the horrible memories of her traumatic childhood experiences that continued to assail her. "I've never had a peaceful day or a night of really restful sleep because of the flashbacks and nightmares I still suffer," she said. "I'm an emotional wreck and my relationships haven't worked, so I know I'm a victim of my past. It's always been hard for me to see peace or happiness ahead."

The sage spent a few silent moments with her before speaking. "You have looked at life as that traumatised child. No wonder it's been so scary and difficult for you. Your freedom begins when you realise that those traumas happened many years ago, they are not happening now. You live as if they are."

The woman nodded in agreement. "That's exactly how it is."

"Freedom from the past is the greatest challenge for all of us, and to the extent we are in the present, we're free," the sage added. "Instead of looking at life through the eyes of a wounded child, can you look through the eyes of a forty year old? Look at your past through those eyes to set yourself free."

Puppet

"Most people claim to be free," said the sage, "but you seldom find a free human being."

"I'm my own master. Nobody controls me," one of the listeners asserted.

"By praising you, do others make you happy? By criticising you, do they make you unhappy?" asked the sage.

"Of course, without a doubt," the man replied.

"Then they have you under control," confirmed the sage.

Sacredness

A man said his wife and he had a reasonably happy married life for fifteen years with several ups and downs. "We made fidelity to the other our first rule and concern for the well-being of the other our paramount obligation. I think that is our secret."

"A close relationship cannot be based on rules and obligations," the sage said. "If your fidelity is to yourself first, you will nurture your own sacredness. That will provide the surest ground for a lasting relationship and ensure you're faithful while remaining truly free."

Beliefs

The sage invited his listeners to examine the beliefs that controlled and limited them. One of them realised that people in her family had failed in business because there was a strong family belief that nobody in the family would ever be rich.

Another had discovered recently that in her family no males lived beyond sixty-five. And she could see the underlying belief that resulted in the death of the males in her family by age sixty-five.

"Beliefs control you. They guide you, limit you and imprison you," said the sage.

"Can beliefs also set you free?" asked one of them.

"Of course," the sage replied, "but only within limits."

Slavery

"Human beings clamour for freedom," said the sage, "but people are quite uneasy when they are in a position to experience it." He added that people are, in fact, afraid of free people and even get rid of them.

"Why?" his listeners wanted to know.

"Because freedom is scary and slavery gives a familiar security," he replied.

Comfort

"Freedom is making peace with the way things are," the sage told a visitor.

"Isn't that a cop out?" the man asked. "Don't we have to do everything in our power to change the world?"

"We certainly do," agreed the sage, "and then you make peace with whatever is."

Enemies

A seeker said that she had tried hard to love her enemies but she had not made much headway.

"You can't love enemies," the sage granted. "When your heart is whole, you are no longer divided between for and against. Then you don't see enemies any longer."

Instrument

In a discussion with a theologian, the sage said, "The greatest freedom is not being able to choose from different options, but to realise that you are an instrument of the divine. The mystic is free, knowing that he does nothing, but everything is done through him."

"That sounds as if I'm just a puppet. I want my freedom," the theologian rejected the sage's idea.

In response the sage told him an Indian story about a swan that flew in from heaven and saw a crane wading on the muddy banks of a little stream in search of snails. He flew over to the crane and started describing the glories of heaven.

The crane was not the least bit interested in the swan's glowing description. "Are there snails in that place?" asked the crane.

"Of course not," the swan replied with conviction.

"Then you can keep your heaven," the crane told him. "I want my snails," he insisted, as he flew in search of his favourite food along the swampy banks.

Destiny

"Our destiny is in our own hands," stated a visitor. "It's ours to decide where we go with it."

"As much as the horse knows the mind of the rider," the sage responded.

"So does that mean we are not free to do what we want in life?" the visitor persisted.

"Of course we are free to do whatever is before us to be done. But what is the value of a freedom where you are free to act but you don't have any control over the consequences?" the sage asked.

Liberation

Serious spiritual seekers questioned the sage about the final freedom he had talked about.

"The ultimate journey into freedom is the one of the dewdrop into the ocean," the sage explained to them.

"Are you referring to our departure from the world?" a seeker asked.

"For one who is free there is no coming and no going," the sage said. "One who is aware is always a dewdrop in the ocean."

About the Author

Dr. Francis Valloor is an author and international speaker. His life long quest brought him in contact with many wonderful spiritual teachers, friends and several masters and sages such as Anthony de Mello. It was he who set him on the path of Awareness. After de Mello's death, Francis worked as the director of Sadhana Institute in Lonavla, India for fourteen years before spending two years as a visiting scholar at the University of Notre Dame. Currently he lives in Dublin, Ireland where he works as a Clinical Psychologist in private practice and conducts Awareness workshops and retreats. He is the author of *A Dewdrop in the Ocean – Wisdom Stories for Turbulent Times* (2009) and *The Ocean in the Dewdrop – Awakening the Sage Within* (2010).

For more information, please visit: www.valloorinstitute.com

About the Artist

The Cover artwork is a detail
of the painting ('Amazing Grace / Oil on Board')
by renowned artist Paul McCloskey from Ireland.

Paul McCloskey was born in Carrickmacross, Co. Monaghan and is now living and working in Gorey Co. Wexford. Paul attended the National College of Art and Design (N.C.A.D) Dublin and De Montfort University UK where he received a Masters Degree in Fine art painting (MFA) in 2010. He has exhibited extensively both nationally and internationally throughout the UK, London, Venice, Paris and New York and he has received multiple awards for his work, which are held in important collections.

To learn more about Paul McCloskey and his work please visit
www.paulmccloskeyart.com